Step by Step

Piano Course

by

Edna Mae Burnam

To Chris, Billy, Mona, Katie, and Matthew

PLAYBACK+
Speed • Pitch • Balance • Loop

To access audio, visit:
www.halleonard.com/mylibrary

Enter Code
6638-7543-0207-2381

ISBN 978-1-4234-3605-8

EXCLUSIVELY DISTRIBUTED BY

WILLIS MUSIC

HAL•LEONARD®

Visit Hal Leonard Online at
www.halleonard.com

Contact us:
Hal Leonard
7777 West Bluemound Road
Milwaukee, WI 53213
Email: info@halleonard.com

In Europe, contact:
Hal Leonard Europe Limited
42 Wigmore Street
Marylebone, London, W1U 2RN
Email: info@halleonardeurope.com

In Australia, contact:
Hal Leonard Australia Pty. Ltd.
4 Lentara Court
Cheltenham, Victoria, 3192 Australia
Email: info@halleonard.com.au

PREFACE

My aim and purpose in presenting *Step by Step* is a sincere hope that it will help every student become aware of the joy that comes in being able to express themselves musically.

Step by Step will help make learning to play the piano a happy and joyous experience.

Step by Step presents the rudiments of music in a logical order, with gradual and steady progress, presenting a challenge toward increasing pianistic facility.

Step by Step provides appealing, melodious music for the student to play, and it keeps this music within the range of the student's ability thereby enabling fluent and artistic performance.

Step by Step further stimulates the student's interest by containing written work in the form of "musical games," thereby giving theory an exciting approach.

Step by Step will help to awaken a deep love for music – the rightful heritage of all.

EDNA MAE BURNAM

TO THE TEACHER

Edna Mae Burnam's *Step by Step Piano Course* is designed to present to the beginning piano student the many subjects they must learn in order to be able to read and play music.

If these subjects are presented too quickly, or too many given at one time, confusion and a distaste for music may result.

This book presents these subjects in their logical order and ONE AT A TIME. Sufficient work is given at each step so that the student will thoroughly comprehend a topic before going on to the next one.

In Book 1, as with those that follow, the subjects dealt with are covered in a clear and complete manner. The musical exercises lie under the hands, and music writing games add to musical knowledge. A final check-up and review ensures complete understanding.

When Book 1 is completed, the student will have learned the following:

1. How the fingers are numbered for piano playing.

2. Learn to recognize and name the following rudiments:

   Treble clef
   Bass clef
   Brace
   Grand staff
   Bar line
   Measure
   Double bar
   Finger markings (fingerings)

3. Learn to name and play the following notes:

4. Learn the number of counts for the following kinds of notes:

5. Learn the number of counts for the following kinds of rests: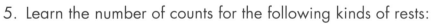

6. Learn to play and count in the following time signatures: $\frac{2}{4}$ $\frac{3}{4}$ $\frac{4}{4}$

7. Learn to play and count a tie correctly.

THIS IS HOW YOU NUMBER YOUR FINGERS FOR PLAYING THE PIANO

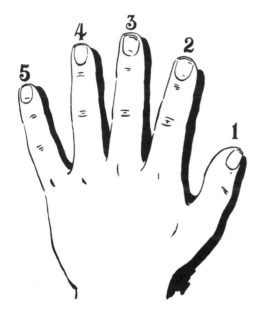

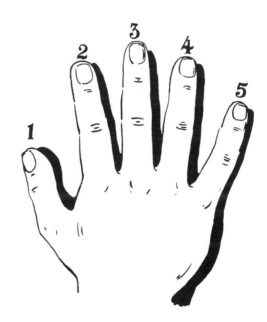

Left hand

Right hand

HERE ARE TWO BLACK KEYS

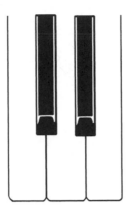

Find them on the piano.

See how many groups of the two black keys you can find.

Play them one at a time and sing "One, Two."

Use any fingers you wish.

MIDDLE C ON KEYBOARD

Find the WHITE note to the left of the two black keys (in the **middle** of the keyboard).

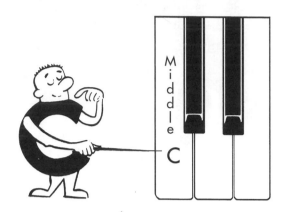

This WHITE note is named MIDDLE C.

Play it with either hand but use your FIRST finger (thumb) as you play MIDDLE C. Sing C as you play it.

TREBLE CLEF

This is a **treble clef** sign

Notes from MIDDLE C to the **top** of the keyboard to the **right,** are written **after** a treble clef sign.

BASS CLEF

This is a **bass clef sign**

Notes from MIDDLE C to the **bottom** of the keyboard to the **left,** are written **after** a bass clef sign.

MIDDLE C's PLAY YARD

MIDDLE C has a wide play yard.

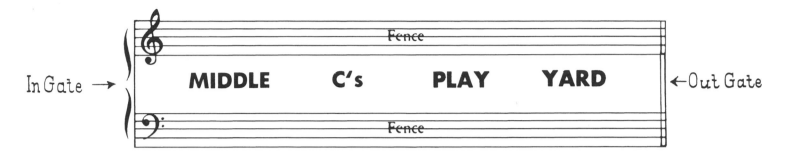

There is a fence on two sides of the play yard.

There is a fancy iron gate to go **into** the play yard.

There is a double bar iron gate at the end.

MIDDLE C **never** goes out of the play yard.

PICTURES OF MIDDLE C

Here are some pictures of MIDDLE C.

MIDDLE C is **always in** the play yard. It may be in different parts of the play yard but it cannot climb on the fences.

MIDDLE C **always** has a line going through it ⟶ 𝅝 (this is called a **leger** line).

Sometimes MIDDLE C has a stem.

The stem may point up or it may point down

MIDDLE C may be white or it may be black

Look below and see the different pictures of MIDDLE C in the play yard.

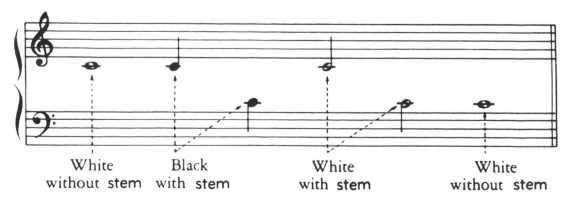

White without stem   Black with stem   White with stem   White without stem

LOOK AT THE PICTURES OF MIDDLE C

Play MIDDLE C just as many times as you see it in the play yard.

Use either hand you wish, but use your **first** finger (thumb).

Begin at the "In Gate" and play each MIDDLE C to the "Out Gate".

Keep your eyes on the MIDDLE C's so that you will not lose your place!

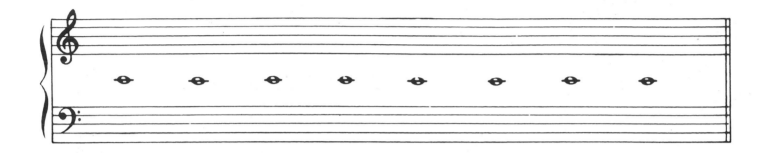

MIDDLE C WITH STEM

Here is a picture of MIDDLE C with a stem pointing **up**

Is the stem on the right or left side of MIDDLE C?

When the stem goes **up,** you must play MIDDLE C with the hand that is on the same **side** as the stem. (Your **right** hand).

Use the **first** finger (thumb) of your **right** hand as you play the MIDDLE C's below.

The number 1 above MIDDLE C is a finger mark. It means to use the first finger of your right hand.

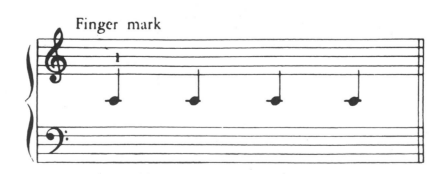

When the stem goes **down,** you must play MIDDLE C with the hand that is on the same side as the stem (your **left** hand).

Use the **first** finger (thumb) of your **left** hand as you play the MIDDLE C's below.

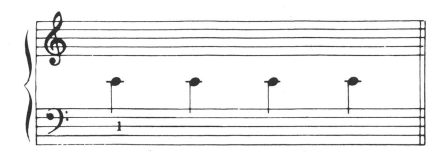

HERE ARE MORE MIDDLE C's

BE SURE YOU PLAY EACH ONE WITH THE CORRECT HAND!

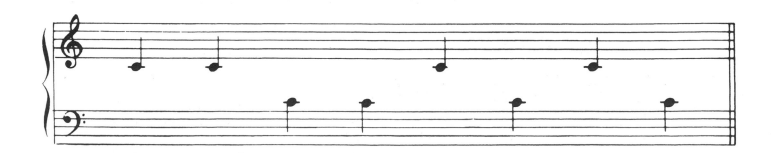

BAR LINES – DOUBLE BAR LINES – MEASURES

There are lines separating MIDDLE C's play yard. In music, these are called **bars.**

The places **between** these bars are called measures.

Notice the last heavy **double bar.** It means we have come to the end.

How many measures are there below?

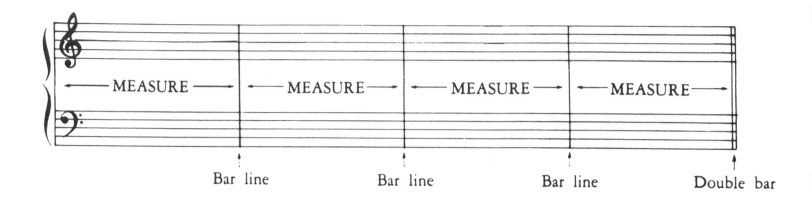

COUNT THREE KINDS OF MIDDLE C's

When MIDDLE C is **black** and has a **stem,** it sings long enough for you to count **ONE.** (This is a **quarter** note).

Play and count 1

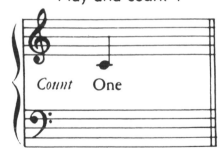

When MIDDLE C is **white** and has a **stem,** it sings a little longer. Long enough for you to count **ONE, TWO.** (This is a **half** note).

Play and count 1, 2

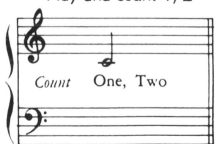

When MIDDLE C is **white** and has no **stem,** it sings even **longer.** Long enough for you to count ONE, TWO, THREE, FOUR. (This is a whole note).

Play and count 1, 2, 3, 4

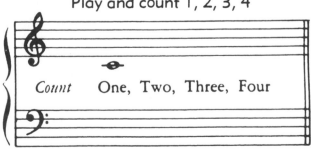

$\frac{2}{4}$ TIME SIGNATURE

Notice the numbers on the fences.

You must remember the one that is on **top.**

What is it?

It means that you must count 1, 2 in **every measure.**

These numbers are called TIME SIGNATURES.

After every **bar** line you must **always** begin counting ONE again.

Clap and **count** for each MIDDLE C below.

Do not stop until you reach the **double bar** at the end.

TIP TOE

Count like this ------> One, Two, | One, Two, | One, Two, | One, Two.

Did you remember to count, ONE, TWO in the last measure?

Now **play** and count. Use correct hands and fingers.

The name of this piece is TIP TOE.

When you can **play** and **count** this piece perfectly, you may sing these words:—

"Tip - toe, Tip - toe, Here I Go".

Now play TIP TOE again and your teacher will play with you.

Teacher's Part

$\frac{4}{4}$ TIME SIGNATURE

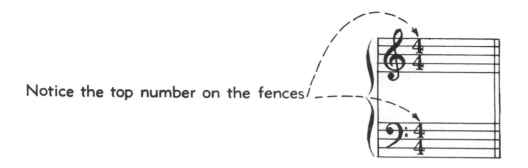

Notice the top number on the fences

This means that you must count 1, 2, 3, 4 in every measure.

Clap and count the piece named HOP and STOP.

When you can play and count it perfectly you may sing the words.

HOP and STOP

Here is another piece for you to learn in the same way.

POP CORN

D ON KEYBOARD

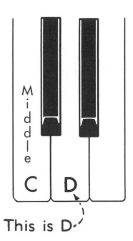

This is D

Find the next note to the **right** of Middle C (**between** the two black keys).

Play D with the **second** finger of your **right** hand.
Sing D as you play it.

Here are some pictures of D.

Remember that D is the note **between** the two black keys.
D does **NOT** have a leger line through it.
D is in Middle C's play yard. It can only play in the **top** of the play yard.
Use the second finger of your right hand to play D.

Here are some pieces for you to play:

SLEEP

Sleep, my ba - by, Sleep.

Teacher's Part

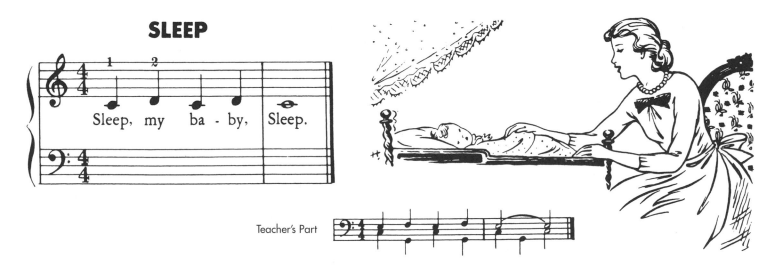

ON THE BUS

On the bus the peo - ple trav - el, All a - round the town.

Teacher's Part

THE RAIN

Hear the gen - tle rain, On the wind - ow - pane.

Teacher's Part

LEAVES

Leaves are fall - ing down, All a - round the town.

Teacher's Part

B ON KEYBOARD

Find the white note
to the **left** of Middle C.

B

This is B

Play B with the **second** finger of your **left** hand.

Sing B as you play it.

16

PICTURES OF B

Here are some pictures of B.

B is in Middle C's play yard. It can only play in the **bottom** of it.

Use the second finger of your **left** hand as you play B.

Here are some new pieces for you to play.

BOAT SONG

Rock my lit - tle boat.

Teacher's Part

THE DRUM

Rub, Dub, Dub, | Rub, Dub, Dub, | Hear me play my | drum.

Teacher's Part

IN A HAMMOCK

Back and forth, and | back and forth, and | back and forth, I'm | swing-ing.

Teacher's Part

Here is a piece named THE WOODPECKER

Notice the third measure.

In this measure the **right** hand plays on counts 1, 2, 3, 4.

The **left** hand plays on counts 1, 2, 3, 4 **also.**

You must play with **both hands at the same time** in this third measure!

THE WOODPECKER

Tap, tap, tap, tap. | Tap, tap, tap, tap. | Tap - ping all day | long.

Teacher's Part

E ON KEYBOARD

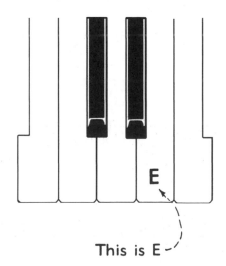

Find the white note to the **right** of D.

E

This is E

Play E with the **third** finger of your **right** hand.

Sing E as you play it.

BRACE – STAFF – GRAND STAFF

The music name for "fence" is **staff.** The **staff** is made up of lines and spaces.

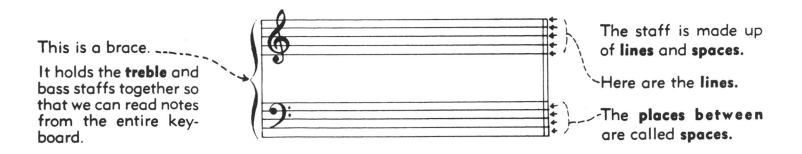

This is a brace. ----

It holds the **treble** and bass staffs together so that we can read notes from the entire keyboard.

The staff is made up of **lines** and **spaces.**

Here are the **lines.**

The **places between** are called **spaces.**

Usually the right hand plays notes written on the treble staff.

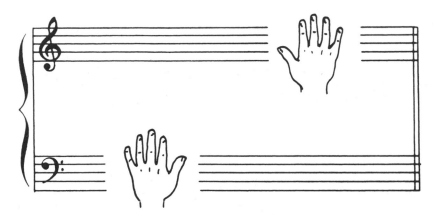

Usually the left hand plays notes written on the bass staff.

PICTURES OF E

Here are some pictures of E.

E is **not** in MIDDLE C's play yard. It is on the **treble** staff.

How many lines make up the treble staff?

E is on the treble staff — on **this** line. _ _ _ _

Play E with the **third finger** of your **right hand.**

Sing E as you play it. Here are some pieces for you to play.

Remember the numbers on the fences!

The **top** one is the one you must remember!

Count 1, 2 in every measure!

SING TO ME

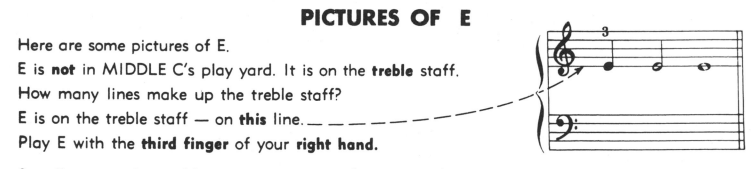

Sing to me, C, D, E!

Teacher's Part

Here is another piece for you to play.

THE SHOE COBBLER

Rap, tap, tap, tap, | Rap, tap, tap, tap, | Cob-bler mend my | shoe.

Teacher's Part

THE RAIN

Pit-ter, pat-ter, | goes the rain,

On the birds and | flowers. | Pit-ter, pat-ter, | goes the rain, | For so man-y | hours.

Teacher's Part

A ON KEYBOARD

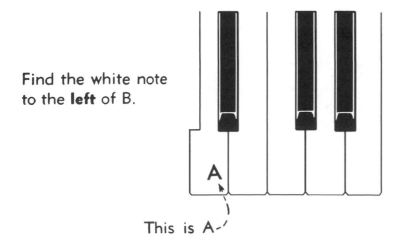

Find the white note to the **left** of B.

This is A

Play A with the **third** finger of your **left** hand.

Sing A as you play it.

A is **not** in MIDDLE C's play yard. It is on the **bass** staff.

How many lines make up the **bass** staff?

A is on the bass staff — on **this** line. ——

Play A with the **third** finger of your **left hand.**

Sing A as you play it.

KITTY CAT

Kit - ty   cat   is | sleep - ing. | Sleep-ing   in   the | sun.

Teacher's Part

IN THE SNOW

Down   I | go, | In   the | snow.

Teacher's Part

TWO   SINGING

Right hand is Mother's voice.
Left   hand   is   Father's voice.

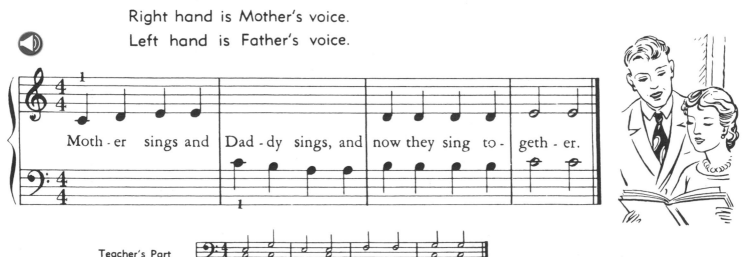

Moth - er   sings and | Dad - dy   sings, and | now they sing to - | geth - er.

Teacher's Part

CROSSING THE CREEK

Here is a little creek. Each circle is a rock. Write the name of each note in the circle.

See if you can cross the creek without getting your feet wet!

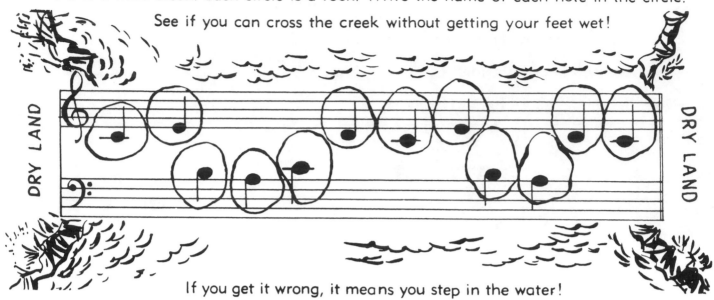

If you get it wrong, it means you step in the water!

BIRTHDAY CAKES

Here are birthday cakes that need candles.

Put as many candles on each cake as there are **counts** in the **notes** on the cake.

A note like this ♩ gets **one** count.   The first one is done to show you how to do the others.

SOLDIERS

Each soldier beats **four measures** on his drum.

The soldier is beating either $\frac{2}{4}$ or $\frac{4}{4}$ time.

Write the **time signature** before each line.

Write the **counts** under each note. Like this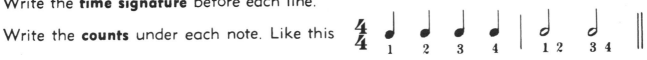

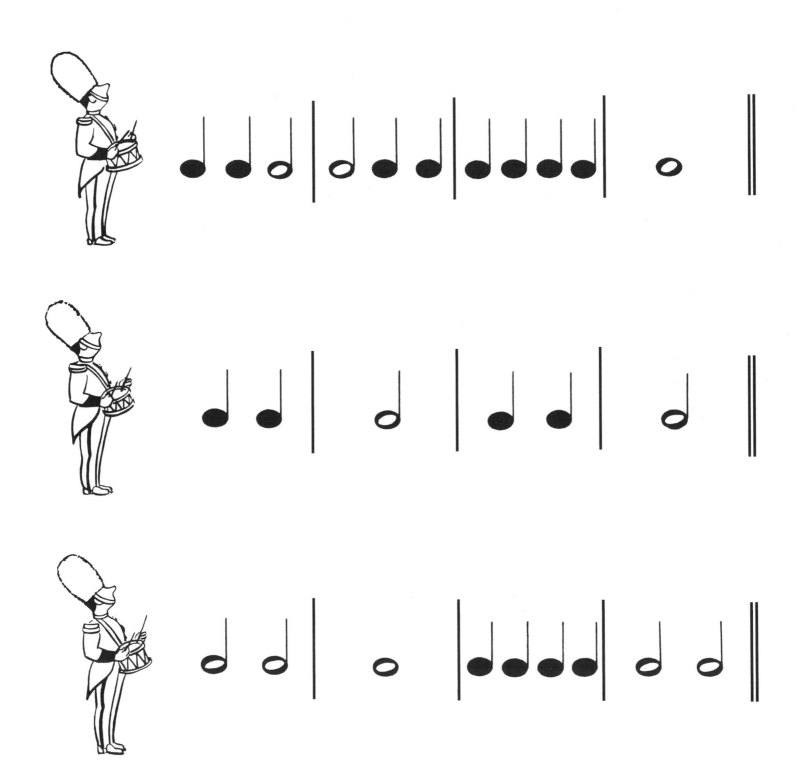

$\frac{3}{4}$ TIME SIGNATURE

You have had pieces
with **two** counts in a measure.

You have had pieces with
four counts in a measure.

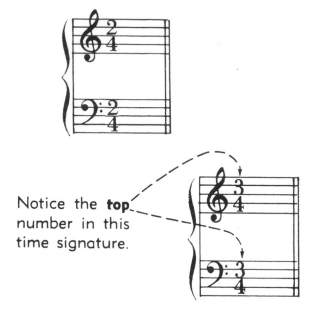

Notice the **top**
number in this
time signature.

This means that you
must count 1, 2, 3 in
each measure.

One, Two, Three

You know that a note like this 𝅗𝅥 sings long enough for you to count 1, 2.

When a note like this has a dot after it 𝅗𝅥.   it sings long enough for you to count 1, 2, 3.

Here are some pieces for you to play.

NORTH WIND

North wind is   blow-ing and   sing-ing   a   song.

Did you remember to count 1, 2, 3 for
the last note?

Teacher's Part

SWIMMING POOL

Swim-ming a - round in a swim-ming pool,

Swim-ming a - round keeps me nice and cool.

Teacher's Part

ICE CREAM CONE

I'd like an ice cream cone. Straw-ber-ry ice cream cone.

Teacher's Part

HOT CROSS BUNS

Hot Cross Buns, Hot Cross Buns! One a pen-ny, Two a pen-ny, Hot Cross Buns!

A TIE

When the same note is pictured **two** times, and they are **tied together** with a curved line like

this ♩⌣♩ or ♩‿♩ this is called a **tie**.

When this happens you must play the **first** note, and **HOLD** the second note and **count** it.

DO NOT LIFT YOUR HAND AND PLAY THE SECOND (or tied) NOTE AGAIN.

Here are some **ties**.

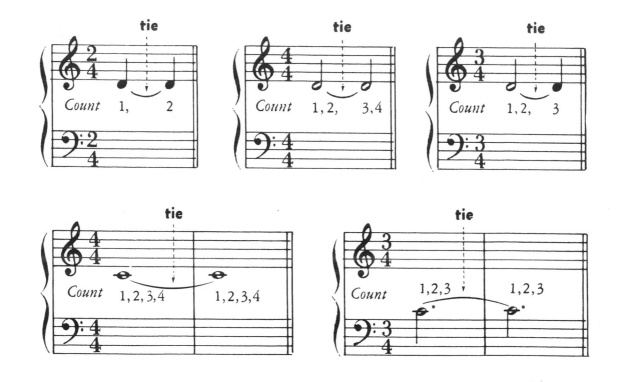

Here are some pieces with **ties**. Point them out.

BOSSY COW

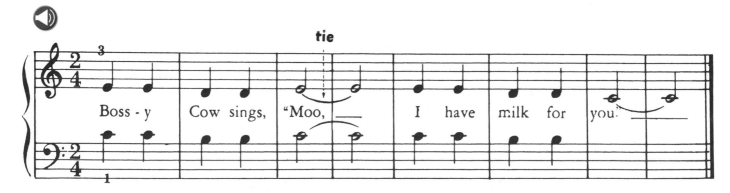

Boss - y Cow sings, "Moo, I have milk for you."

Point out the **ties** in the Teacher's part.

Teacher's Part

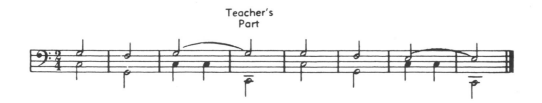

GOLDFISH

Gold-fish swim a-round, and round, and round.

Gold-fish nev-er, nev-er make a sound.

Teacher's Part

SNOWY WHITE CLOUDS

Snow-y white clouds in the sky,— Sail-ing by.—

Teacher's Part

RESTS

A **rest** is a sign of silence.

A **one** count rest: This kind of rest gets **ONE** count.

This is a **quarter** rest.

When you see a rest sign, you must lift your hand from the keyboard and count the rest.

Here is a piece that has some one count rests:

JUMP ROPE

Count   1,   2,   3,   4

Your hands do **not** always rest at the same time.
Sometimes they **take turns** resting.

Play the piece below:

HOP SCOTCH

TWO COUNT RESTS

This kind of rest gets **two** counts.

It sits on the **middle** line of each staff.

This is a **half** rest.

Here is a piece that has some two count rests.

ROCKING CHAIR

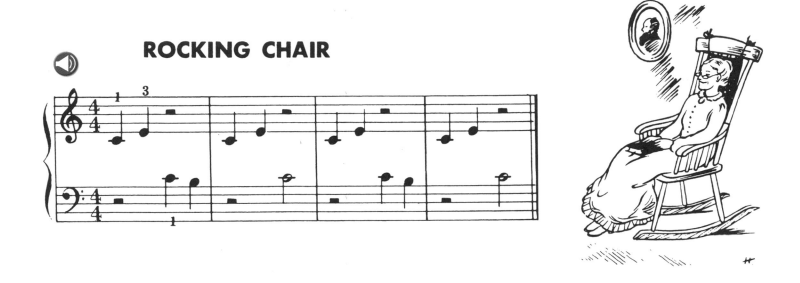

This piece has some **one** count rests and also some **two** count rests.

BUMPY STREETS

FOUR COUNT RESTS

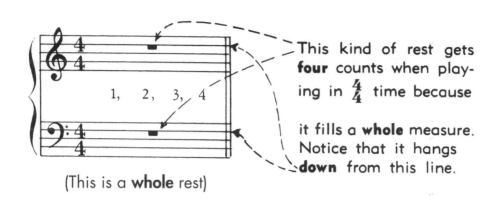

This kind of rest gets **four** counts when play-ing in $\frac{4}{4}$ time because

it fills a **whole** measure. Notice that it hangs **down** from this line.

(This is a **whole** rest)

When playing in $\frac{3}{4}$ time this same kind of rest gets **three** counts because it fills the whole measure.

(Whole rest)

SHEEP

Sheep are stand-ing on a hill, and they stand ver-y still.

WHEELS

Wheels go a - round and a - round___ Wheels go all o - ver the ground.___

Did you remember to count this tie?

Here is a piece that has **all** of the different kinds of rests you have learned.

MAIL MAN

32

F ON KEYBOARD

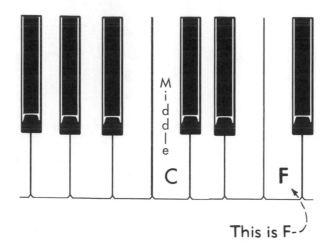

Middle C

F

This is F--

Find the white note to the **right** of E.

Here are some pictures of F.

F is **not** in MIDDLE C's play yard.

It is on the **treble** staff.

Remember that the places **between** the lines are called **spaces.**

How many spaces are on the treble staff?

F is on the treble staff and in **this** space. —

Play F with the **fourth** finger of your **right** hand.

Sing F as you play it.

Here is a piece for you to play.

THE NIGHT

When I go out - side and look in - to the night,

I can see the stars, All beau - ti - ful and bright.

CORN ON THE COB

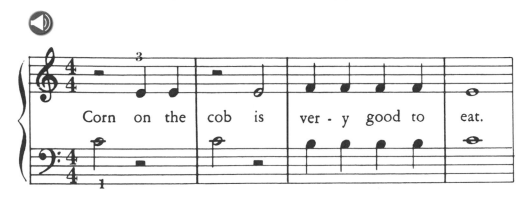

Corn on the cob is ver-y good to eat.

Nib-ble, nib-ble, nib-ble, Eve-ry bite is sweet.

ROCK-A-BYE DOLLY

Rock-a-bye Dol-ly, I love you true. I sure-ly hope that you love me, too!

G BELOW MIDDLE C – ON KEYBOARD

Find the
white note
to the **left**
of A.
(Below MIDDLE C)

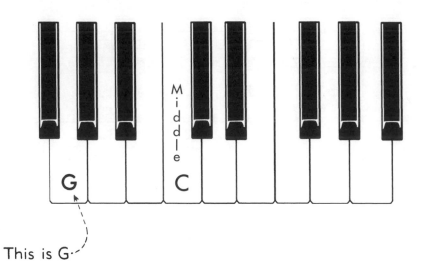

This is G

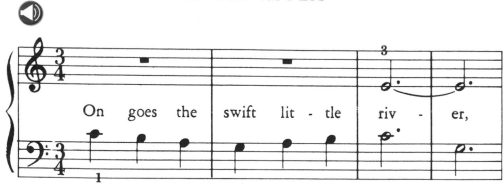

Play G with the **fourth** finger of your **left** hand.

Sing G as you play it.

Here are some pictures of G for the **left** hand.

This G is on the **bass** staff.

It is on **this** space of the bass staff.

LITTLE RIVER

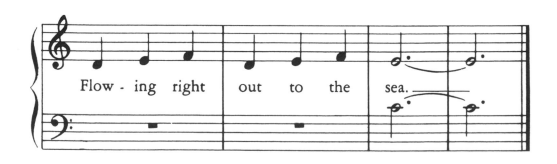

On goes the swift lit - tle riv - er,

Flow - ing right out to the sea.

EVENING

In the ear - ly eve - ning shad - ows fall.

I like ear - ly eve - ning best of all.

LONDON BRIDGE

Traditional

Lon - don bridge is fall - ing down, Fall - ing down, Fall - ing down,

Lon - don bridge is fall - ing down, My Fair Lad - y - o.

G ABOVE MIDDLE C – ON KEYBOARD

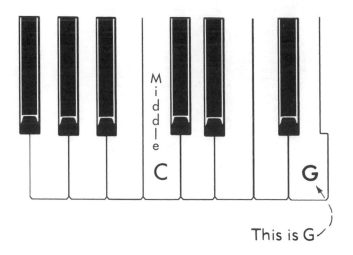

This is G

Find the white note
to the **right** of F (above Middle C).

Here are some pictures of G
for the **right** hand.

It is on **this** line of the **treble** staff.

Play this G with the **fifth** finger of your **right** hand.

Sing G as you play it.

HILLS

Hills go up and hills go down all

in and out the cit - y. Hills go up and hills go down, and they are ver-y pret-ty.

TV ANTENNAS

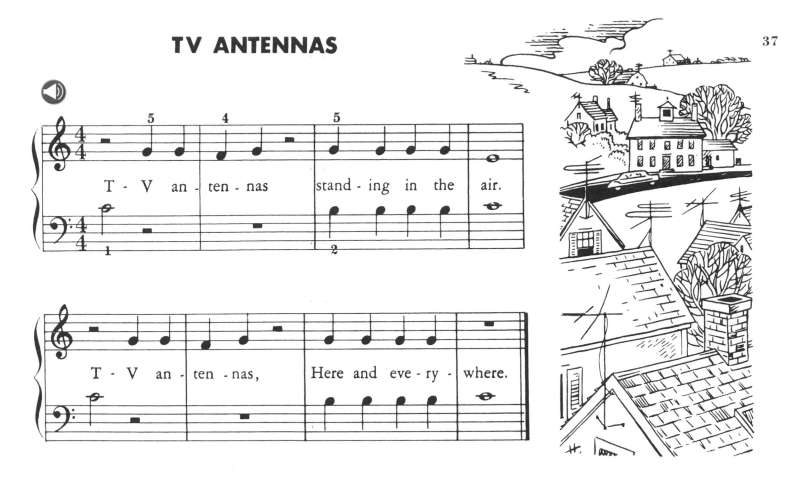

T - V an - ten - nas standing in the air.

T - V an - ten - nas, Here and eve - ry - where.

MARY HAD A LITTLE LAMB

Traditional

Mar - y had a lit - tle lamb, lit - tle lamb, lit - tle lamb.

Mar - y had a lit - tle lamb, Its fleece was white as snow.

TWO CHILDREN HUMMING

Lit - tle chil - dren hum - ming, hum - ming, hum - ming,

Lit - tle chil - dren hum - ming, all day long.

SUNSET

When the sun sets way down low,

Beau - ti - ful and bright. When the sun sets then I know, It is near - ly night.

FISHING

Draw a fishing line from each pole to the fish it should catch.

If the pole is marked C, the line must go to the note C.

If you get it right, it means you caught the fish!

See how many fish (notes) you can catch.

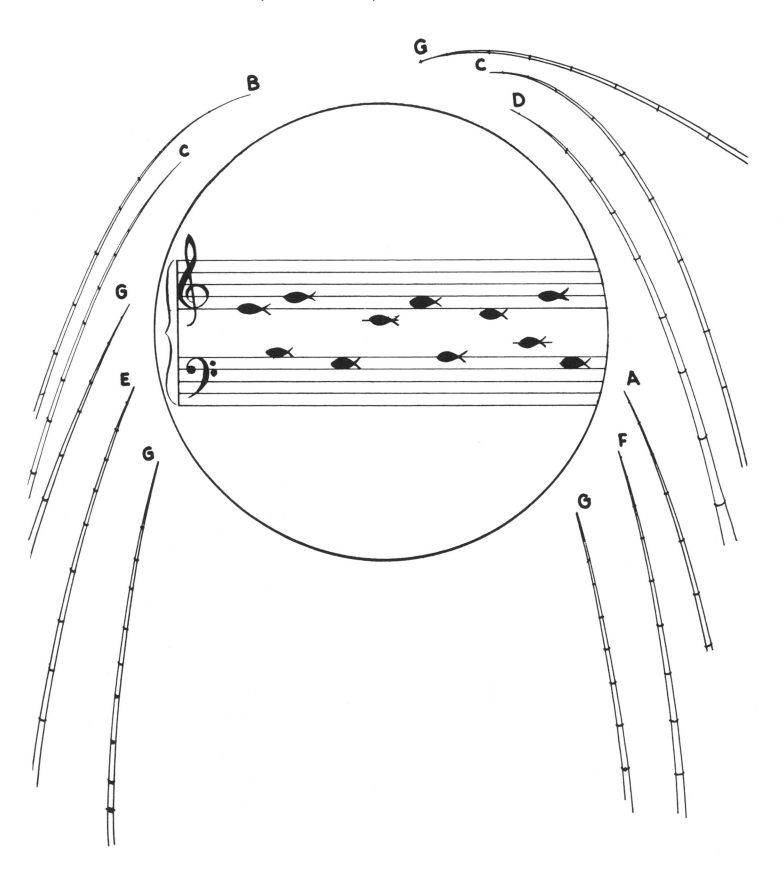

PENNIES IN A PURSE

Each purse has pennies inside it.

How many pennies are there in each purse?

There are as many pennies as there are counts in the notes.

Write the number of counts in each purse.

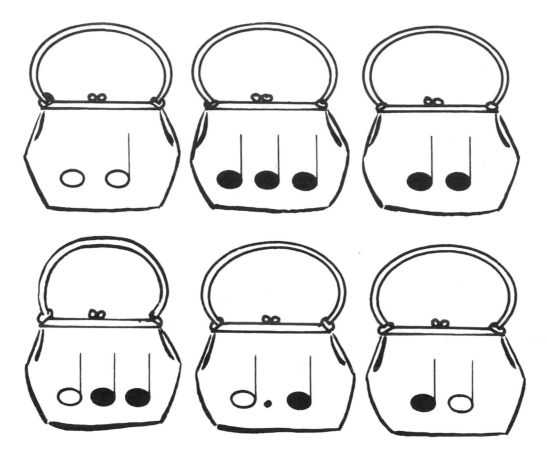

This time count the **notes and rests.**

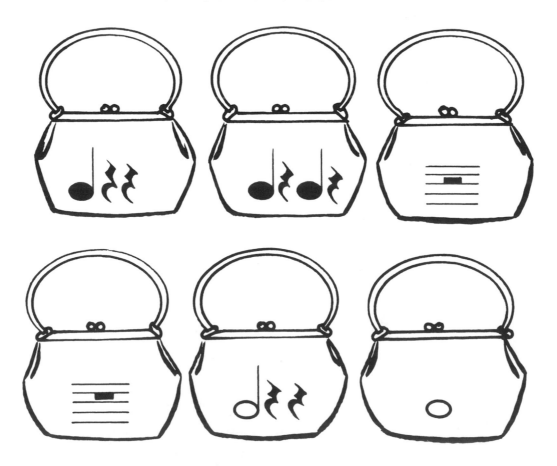

DUCKS

Each duck quacks four measures.

They quack in either $\frac{2}{4}$, $\frac{3}{4}$ or $\frac{4}{4}$ time.

Write the correct time signature before each line.

Then write the counts under the notes or rests.

Like this:

LITTLE WHITE CHICKENS

Lit - tle white chick - ens in Grand - moth - er's yard,

All the day long they keep peck - ing ver - y hard.

SOUTH WIND

High up in the tall - est tree,

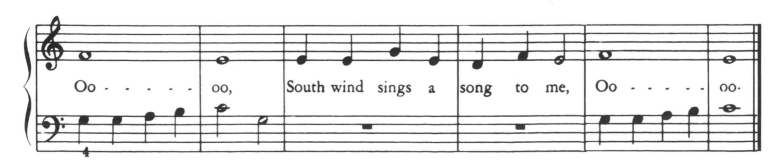

Oo - - - - oo, South wind sings a song to me, Oo - - - - oo.

HIGHWAYS

Highways go just everywhere, On hills and deserts, too.

Countries, cities, everywhere, and by the sea so blue.

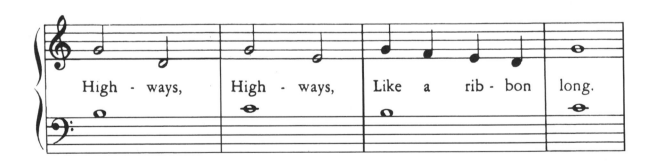

Highways, Highways, Like a ribbon long.

Highways, Highways, Beautiful and strong.

FINAL CHECK-UP

Your teacher will give you this final check-up.

- Tell me how your fingers are numbered for playing the piano.

- Show me a:

    Treble clef
    Bass clef
    Grand staff
    Bar line
    Measure
    Double bar
    Brace
    Time Signature

- Show me a note that gets:

    1 count
    2 counts
    3 counts
    4 counts

- Show me a rest that gets:

    1 count
    2 counts
    4 counts

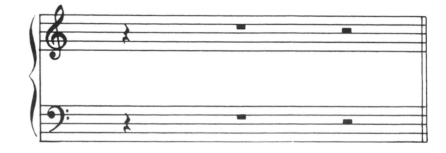

- Show me a time signature that means:

    2 counts to each measure
    4 counts to each measure
    3 counts to each measure

- Show me a tie:

Certificate of Merit

This certifies that

....

has successfully completed

BOOK ONE
OF
EDNA MAE BURNAM'S
PIANO COURSE

STEP BY STEP

and is eligible for promotion to

BOOK TWO

....

Teacher

....

Date

A DOZEN A DAY

by Edna Mae Burnam

The **A Dozen A Day** books are universally recognized as one of the most remarkable technique series on the market for all ages! Each book in this series contains short warm-up exercises to be played at the beginning of each practice session, providing excellent day-to-day training for the student. All book/audio versions include orchestrated accompaniments by Ric Ianonne.

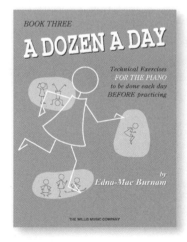

MINI BOOK
00404073 Book Only $5.99
00406472 Book/Audio $9.99

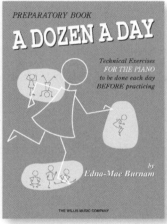

PREPARATORY BOOK
00414222 Book Only $5.99
00406476 Book/Audio $9.99

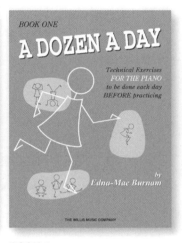

BOOK 1
00413366 Book Only $5.99
00406481 Book/Audio $9.99

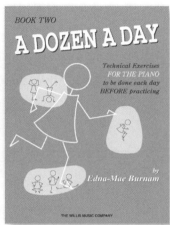

BOOK 2
00413826 Book Only $5.99
00406485 Book/Audio $9.99

BOOK 3
00414136 Book Only $6.99
00416760 Book/Audio $10.99

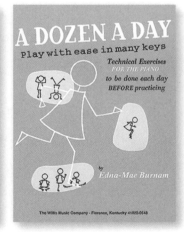

BOOK 4
00415686 Book Only $6.99
00416761 Book/Audio $10.99

**PLAY WITH EASE
IN MANY KEYS**
00416395 Book Only $5.99

**A DOZEN A DAY
ANTHOLOGY**
00158307 Book/Audio $24.99

ALSO AVAILABLE:

The **A Dozen A Day Songbook** series containing Broadway, movie, and pop hits!

Visit Hal Leonard Online at **www.halleonard.com**

WILLIS MUSIC

EXCLUSIVELY DISTRIBUTED BY

HAL•LEONARD®

Prices, contents, and availability subject to change without notice. Prices listed in U.S. funds.

Edna Mae Burnam was a pioneer in piano publishing. The creator of the iconic *A Dozen a Day* technique series and *Step by Step* method was born on September 15, 1907 in Sacramento, California. She began lessons with her mother, a piano teacher who drove a horse and buggy daily through the Sutter Buttes mountain range to reach her students. In college Burnam decided that she too enjoyed teaching young children, and majored in elementary education at California State University (then Chico State College) with a minor in music. She spent several years teaching kindergarten in public schools before starting her own piano studio and raising daughters Pat and Peggy. She delighted in composing for her students, and took theory and harmony lessons from her husband David (a music professor and conductor of the Sacramento Symphony in the 1940s).

Burnam began submitting original pieces to publishers in the mid-1930s, and was thrilled when one of them, "The Clock That Stopped," was accepted, even though her remuneration was a mere $20. Undaunted, the industrious composer sent in the first *A Dozen a Day* manuscript to her Willis editor in 1950, complete with stick-figure sketches for each exercise. Her editor loved the simple genius of the playful artwork resembling a musical technique, and so did students and teachers: the book rapidly blossomed into a series of seven and continues to sell millions of copies. In 1959, the first book in the *Step by Step* series was published, with hundreds of individual songs and pieces along the way, often identified by whimsical titles in Burnam's trademark style.

The immense popularity of her books solidified Edna Mae Burnam's place and reputation in music publishing history, yet throughout her lifetime she remained humble and effervescent. "I always left our conversations feeling upbeat and happy," says Kevin Cranley, Willis president. "She could charm the legs off a piano bench," Bob Sylva of the *Sacramento Bee* wrote, "make a melody out of a soap bubble, and a song out of a moon beam."

Burnam died in 2007, a few months shy of her 100th birthday. "Music enriches anybody's life, even if you don't turn out to be musical," she said once in an interview. "I can't imagine being in a house without a piano."